Lives and Times

Thomas Edison

Jane Shuter

Heinemann
LIBRARY

www.heinemann.co.uk
Visit our website to find out more information about Heinemann Library books.

To order:
☎ Phone 44 (0) 1865 888066
▤ Send a fax to 44 (0) 1865 314091
▭ Visit the Heinemann Bookshop at www.heinemann.co.uk to browse our catalogue and order online.

First published in Great Britain by Heinemann Library,
Halley Court, Jordan Hill, Oxford OX2 8EJ,
a division of Reed Educational and Professional Publishing Ltd.
Heinemann is a registered trademark of Reed Educational and Professional Publishing Ltd.

OXFORD MELBOURNE AUCKLAND JOHANNESBURG BLANTYRE
GABORONE IBADAN PORTSMOUTH NH (USA) CHICAGO

© Reed Educational and Professional Publishing Ltd 2002

The moral right of the proprietor has been asserted.

Designed by Visual Image
Illustrations by Sam Thompson
Originated by Dot Gradations Ltd
Printed and bound by South China Printing in Hong Kong/China

ISBN 0 431 13451 0 (hardback)
06 05 04 03 02
10 9 8 7 6 5 4 3 2 1

ISBN 0 431 13456 1 (paperback)
06 05 04 03 02
10 9 8 7 6 5 4 3 2 1

British Library Cataloguing in Publication Data

Shuter, Jane
Thomas Edison. – (Lives and times) (Take-off!)
1. Edison, Thomas A. (Thomas Alva), 1847–1931 – Juvenile literature 2. Electric engineers – United States – Biography – Juvenile literature 3. Inventors – United States – Biography – Juvenile literature
I. Title
621.3'092

Acknowledgements

The publishers would like to thank the following for permission to reproduce photographs: US Department of the Interior, National Park Service, Edison National Historic Site: pp16, 17, 18, 19, 20, 21, 22; Henry Ford Museum and Greenfield Village: p23.

Cover photograph reproduced with permission of Rex Features.

Every effort has been made to contact copyright holders of any material reproduced in this book. Any omissions will be rectified in subsequent printings if notice is given to the publishers.

Contents

Any words appearing in the text in bold,
like this, are explained in the Glossary.

Early life

Thomas Alva Edison was born in Milan, Ohio, USA on 11 February 1847. He had **scarlet fever** as a boy, which made him partly deaf.

Pictures of Thomas, his parents and his family home.

Thomas

Thomas's home

father

mother

passenger

Thomas

Thomas's first job was to sell newspapers on trains.

Edison loved doing **experiments**, finding out
how things worked and trying to improve them.
But he started to work when he was twelve.

Thomas worked as a newsboy on the Grand Trunk
Railway, which linked the USA with Canada.

Working and inventing

In 1862 Edison was taught to use the **telegraph**.
He worked as a telegraph operator at night.

Thomas working as a telegraph operator.

customer

Thomas

telegraph

Edison sold his first **patent** when he was 23. It was for a machine that sent **stock prices** by telegraph.

Thomas thought he would get $3000 for this machine. In fact he got $40,000!

This stock ticker machine sent stock prices by telegraph.

Thomas

stock ticker machine

New Jersey

Edison started a business in Newark, New Jersey. His first job was to improve the **telegraph**. He also **patented** 1093 of his own inventions.

Edison's workshop at Newark, New Jersey

workshop

Alexander Bell patented the telephone while Edison was still working on the idea. But Edison made the **design** better so people could talk over hundreds of kilometres, and not just a few.

Edison and his family.

wife

Thomas

children

Menlo Park

In 1876 Edison moved his business to Menlo Park, near New York. In 1878 he **patented** the **phonograph**.

Edison stayed at Menlo Park from 1876 to 1887. Work out how long he was there.

Edison's workers

Two of his workers made the first phonograph. Edison said, 'This machine's going to talk.' He recited 'Mary had a little lamb' into it. The machine played it back.

Thomas reciting into the phonograph.

phonograph

Thomas

Electric light

On 21 October 1879, Edison and his team tested the electric light bulb. They lit up the whole **laboratory**.

Edison formed a company with an Englishman, Joseph Swan.

Edison put on a public show, which was a huge success.

electric power station

The first **electric power** station in England.

Edison and his team then had to find a way to
make a lot of electric power safely.

Edison set up the first electric
power station in England in 1882.

Later inventions

Edison's kinetoscope was one of the earliest moving-picture cameras (for making films). He used it in a building on wheels, which moved to follow the sun across the sky!

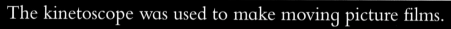
The kinetoscope was used to make moving picture films.

kinetoscope

actors

This first moving picture studio was called 'the Black Maria'.

Thomas Edison photographers

Edison opening the Henry Ford Museum.

In October 1929 Edison opened a museum set up by Henry Ford, another inventor. There was a **replica** of Edison's Menlo Park **laboratory** at the museum.

Edison retired to New Jersey and died on 18 October 1931.

Photographs

There are many ways we can find out about Thomas Edison and his inventions. Photos show us what he and his family looked like.

Thomas married for a second time after his first wife died.

Thomas and his family.

Thomas

There are also photos of Edison's many inventions, and even photos of his workers!

Edison employed 300 people at his Newark workshop.

This photograph of 1876 shows Edison's workers outside the Newark workshop.

workshop

Written clues

Newspapers wrote about Edison's most exciting inventions. Other written records include lists of the films he made, and adverts for his inventions.

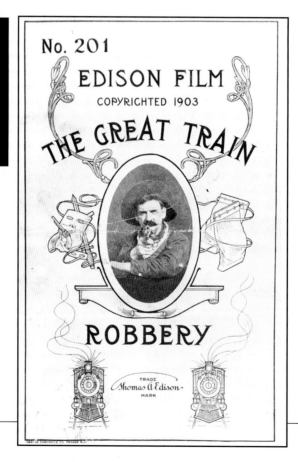

No. 201
EDISON FILM
COPYRIGHTED 1903
THE GREAT TRAIN
ROBBERY

TRADE
Thomas A Edison
MARK

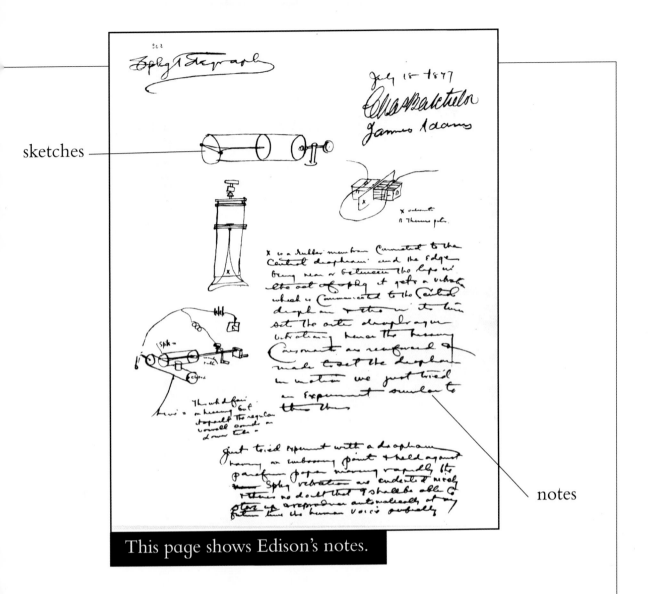

sketches

notes

This page shows Edison's notes.

Edison used workbooks to sketch his ideas and work out inventions. He filled 3400 workbooks, each with 200 pages.

Inventions

Some museums have Edison's inventions on show.

Did you know that Edison was referred to as 'the wizard of Menlo Park'?

This is one of the first phonographs, an early record player.

phonograph

This is one of Edison's first kinetographs. This was his name for moving-picture cameras.

Edison's first film showed one of his workers acting a sneeze.

One of Edison's earliest kinetographs.

Museums

Several museums have displays about Edison. This is the Edison museum in West Orange, New Jersey. Edison retired here, and he built a workshop so he could keep on inventing.

The Edison Museum in West Orange, New Jersey.

museum

Edison's home in West Orange was called Glenmont. It had 23 rooms.

The replica of Menlo Park.

This is a **replica** of Menlo Park in the Henry Ford Museum, Dearborn, Michigan. Everything is copied exactly from Edison's buildings. The real buildings were not strong enough to be moved.

Glossary

This glossary explains difficult words and helps you to say words which may be hard to say.

design drawings of what something will look like and how it will work

experiment trying out ideas to see what happens

laboratory place where people do experiments

patent when a person has a good idea they can go to the patent office, where the idea is given a date and a special number. No one else can use the idea to make money. You say *pay-tent*.

phonograph machine for playing back sounds recorded on a flat disc. You say *fone-a-graf*.

power station place where enough energy is made to run a whole city and sometimes the countryside around as well

replica copy of something that is made to look exactly like it. You say *rep-lick-a*.

scarlet fever sickness which causes very high temperatures and can affect eyesight and hearing

stock price stocks are a small share in a business. The company sells you stocks, then, if they make a profit, you get a share of the profit. The prices of stocks go up and down.

telegraph machine that sends messages over long distances, letter by letter. You say *tell-a-graf*.

Index